I0829807

CONTENTS

LEGAL DISCLAIMER

INTRO

I am a seasoned rideshare driver and mentor. I have given Tens of thousands of rides over the past four years. In this guide I will give you tips on how you can make the most of this job, maximize your revenue and keep your rating solid. In this book you will find the tips and tricks
on how to do so.
This type of job is not a long-term career solution, this is a gig, and you need to consider that when you start. Buying an expensive car will not make the company or passengers love you enough to justify the expense unless it is for a premium service. The company you are working for is almost externally hiring, which means new drivers hit the road almost everyday. Income can be spotty if you aren't clever. It is no longer as simple as turning on the app and waiting.
The first term you want to learn is "pax". It means "passenger". Pax is commonly used for passenger in the airline industry.
This guide was written for everyone getting into ridesharing, from taxi, limo, to customer service agent wishing to be successful in this field. By following the simple instructions in this reference guide you can worker smarter, not harder.

SIGN-UP BONUSES

Most new drivers will qualify for a bonus by signing up for rideshare apps. The Sign on Bonus will ALWAYS vary from city to city, often you can get a better bonus by using a seasoned drivers referral code. Join our Rideshare page or 5 star driver facebook group to connect for a bonus code.
You MUST use the code at sign-up! Rideshare companies do not like to make them retroactive. While it may be possible, it is generally not the rule.

RIDESHARE INSURANCE

Rideshare insurance can protect you and your vehicle while you are online but without a passenger. Some policies cover all 3 periods. Some do not. It is important to understand your personal policy may not cover you if they find out you are driving your car as a commercial operation and stating you drive the car for pleasure. It is insurance fraud, and insurance companies will look for any way to NOT pay if they can, so, rideshare insurance is highly recommended. Remember the deductable from the rideshare companies insurance is anywhere from $1000-$2500 for ANY claim you make! For a comprehensive list of companies that offer rideshare coverage state by state please join our **"5 Star Driver "** Facebook Group.

BUY, OR, RENT A CAR?

Wow Great! I can use my own car! Or can I? The first point is of course about the vehicle. Over the last few years' rideshare companies have become super-rich off not only your labor, but also your investment into your vehicle. Many drivers only see the fare amount and forget that things like gas; wear and tear can significantly bring these numbers down. Depending on how you drive it, you can bring home good pay or you can below minimum wage at times. In this guide we will later go over strategy to avoid that.

Check with your rideshare company about vehicle solutions or partner rentals first! DON'T buy a car, especially brand new solely for rideshare without trying out this gig first! You need to ensure it is profitable enough in your area first to cover more than just the payments and upkeep.

When I first started, until this very day, I rented a car to use. I rented it from a private party online through a website posting. It was a flat $700 payment per month, it was a Prius hybrid, and the only thing I had to pay was the gas and oil. I had to ensure I was on the owner's insurance declaration page for the company to accept it.

In one instance, I took out my own policy and just added the owners name to the entire insurance policy.

Driving full-time the car needed an oil change every month at the very least. But the rest of the expenses fell to the owner once it was returned. Now some may say, that is not right. However that is exactly what the rideshare companies are doing to you, expect they are not funding anything besides the app. The companies are making millions without providing or maintaining a fleet of cars. Instead they have contracted to use yours.

Now some of you cannot/do not want to rent a car, and have our own car you would like to use.

If this is your only option the first word of caution is do you own it?

Or is it financed?

If you own it free and clear, obviously it is your car. If you make payments on the car, shocker: you do not own the car. Therefore it is up to the permission of your lien holder or lender on whether they will allow you to use it for ridesharing and most will say no. The reasoning is: When you take out a personal auto loan you sign a contract. You agree not to abuse or excessively devalue the vehicle.

A lot of lenders consider this gig commercial use of the vehicle and against the terms of the loan. They therefore have the right to

repossess the car if you do not comply. So do check with your
lender before signing yourself up for a nightmare.
There are lease options now from rideshare companies in certain
markets. These might be a better option if you plan to do this
fulltime and don't want to destroy your car.

WHAT KIND OF CAR?

Check with your local regulations before you buy a car first. For
example the state of Nevada requires a business license at the time
of publishing and if you cannot get the license, you cannot drive.
New York CITY is one of the most regulated markets and
requires: commercial insurance, commercial license plates and
commercial TNC drivers license. You cannot put Commercial
plates on MOST financed vehicles unless you either own it, or it is
a commercial loan, or the lender approves which is rare.
Use a hybrid car or high MPG car if you can. Unless it is a
premium service, to use a gas or petrol only vehicle will severely
cut info your profit margins.
Period. Also the cost of repairs is something you want to keep on
the low end. Passengers like a nice roomy backseat, and to get to
their destination in a timely matter. For the lower end services, use
a lower end car. Do not be the person driving the MBZ S-Class
sedan for $1 a mile. Use a sensible car like a Toyota Camry or
Honda
Accord Hybrid.
If you are buying a used car do not spend a lot on it. But
something under 15K that still is within a few years of your
markets cut off so you get some good miles out of it. Doing this
job full time will wear out a car quickly, in about 2-3 years if even
that long. To make the most out of this and not kill your car,
airport trips in the AM take the least amount of wear on your car
as most of it is highway/freeway driving.
The bottom line is this is a commercial operation. Your city may
not have all the regulations in place yet but when they do, you will
be required to adhere to the guidelines. So it's best to start out
ready.

Be ready to buy commercial auto insurance if needed. Be ready to change your personal auto loan to commercial or livery loan when needed. The fines for not following the law can be pretty steep, and rideshare companies have not been all that great as far as advising you what is what. It is up to you to know the rules and regulations.

PRESENTATION OF YOUR CAR

Your car should always, always be clean. Clean the interior and exterior before you take off everyday. Make sure all personal effects are out of sight. Make sure any trade dress, TNC license or stickers are where they are supposed to be according to your market.

A monthly carwash membership is a great investment. For a flat fee you can wash your car multiple times. But be a good customer and buy the same pass the taxi and limo drivers do. Otherwise, down the line, you either be forced to buy one or be turned away from monthly membership. Using the consumer pass on a commercial vehicle is a

No-no most places because you are a commercial vehicle.

I used to vacuum my interior and spray my carpet with febreeze to keep any odors away. I put all season floor mats in the car, which I covered with the regular floor mats. I washed my car in my driveway to cut costs.

After I finished each ride, I always would look in the back to see if there were any left behind items or if the floor was noticeably dirty.

If it appeared so, I would jump out and shake off the floor mat quickly and then resume normal service. Remember, You want clients to feel like you are coming just for them, everyone wants to feel special, so keep a clean car.

Products that I keep in my trunk are: Garbage bags, Leather cleaner/conditioner, Vinyl Seat Covers (easy to clean), tire shine gel will keep your tires looking brand new, window cleaner, surface cleaner with amoral and microfiber towels. Make sure your car is free of dents or needed repairs or you can be taken

offline until it is fixed, do not wait for inspection time as any rider
can anonymously report you if something is missing or broken.

WATER AND CANDY

I started with a box of candy and water for the passenger. Sure
riders loved both, but the candy I found was best for the late night
drunks. It kept some really loud people quiet during the ride. I
recommend at least having some in your trunk in case you decided
to drive late nights.

Daytime passengers usually appreciate the gesture of the water and
about half of them will consume one. You can get a case of 35
bottles for $4 at a wholesale or super store.

Just by keeping it in the car, it ups your service level. If you drive
only at night, take the water out of the car during the day if you
live in a hot climate, no one likes hot water. Tepid or room
temperature water is perfectly fine; most people who open it are
thirsty so it goes down easier.

A good thing to remember is that you are responsible for any items
the pax consumes in your car that you give them. If they start
choking or it causes an emergency, it's going to be on you. It is
your car and your responsibility legally.

CITY KNOWLEDGE

In some cities, you will need to take a city knowledge test. In
some, you will not. Either way, you really should know the major
points of interest of the city, asking the passengers for directions is
COMPLETELY unprofessional!

If you are in a new city, spend your downtime studying the city,
the major routes and traffic flow. It is imperative to your business
operations. Know the bars, clubs, major hotels, places to eat etc.
Ask Passengers you are dropping off in the evening where they are
headed, out, this way you will know where people need rides later.
Know where they are and how far the airport is from where you
are.

You never know when someone is going to jump into the car and tell you "my flight is in 60 minutes!" while this may seem like enough time, if they have a bag to check, it totally isn't. Airport baggage cutoff times are 45 minutes-1 hour before the flight in most airports. At DFW it is one hour. Never deny the pax and tell them you cannot get there. Get them there as fast as you can. It was their responsibility to check their flight time etc. If they miss the flight because they called a car at the last minute, it is their fault not yours. It is not worth a speeding ticket to get them there. Just be as expedient as possible when the passenger says they are late. These are situations where knowing the city and its traffic shortcuts will benefit you greatly.

NAVIGATION

Most of us do not know every single bar, club or restaurant where we live. Use a navigation system that works best for you. Most people use Google maps or Waze. Always ask the pax if they have a preferred route. Some will and some wont, But if they do try to follow it and not argue your points. They are paying you, and if their way turns out to be a disaster, it won't fall onto you. Make sure you have an ENDING point/address or point BEFORE you put the car into drive. Passengers can fall asleep during the ride and you don't want to end up taking them to the wrong place. Many places have 56th st. ne, sw, se, nw. That is 4 different possibilities.
Once you have confirmed the drop-off point, you can start the trip. Ensuring your have the address entered before you take off ensures that you will take your pax to their requested destination without issues along the way. Make sure to check everyday for road closures and special events that may cause traffic jams and find the alternate routes.
Always read the address to the pax! This way you are always sure you have the correct rider, going to the correct place.
If a Passenger requires multiple stops they can be added in their rider app. They can also change the destination en-route. You can show the rider how to do it, but do not change it on your end. This

protects you from rider complaints of fraud or saying you took
them to the wrong place if it comes from their device, no matter
the story, make sure it is done from their phone even if you have to
pull over to show them how. If they are genuine, they will
appreciate it.

TRAFFIC TIPS

Moving violations are your enemy. Too many moving violations
are the quickest exit to this gig. Try to get your moving violations
reduced to non-moving, even if you have to pay a lawyer. The cost
of the lawyer is worth it compared to the insurance cost increases
over time as well as getting deactivated from your platform.

Before starting your trip make sure you know where the PAX is
going and make sure everything is set. Check traffic conditions
quickly for longer trips to make sure you do not get stuck into
construction, remember, mileage is what pays, not time. Make sure
the route and destination is correct before you start the trip to
avoid any possible problems. If you have a bad feeling,
independent contracts can decline the ride.

AUX CABLE AND PHONE CHARGERS

The Aux cable is so the pax can play their music in your car.
Personally, I feel I am the driver so I need to be comfortable. I
never let the passenger control the climate or radio. I never carried
any aux cable for the pax. This is a personal decision you can
make, along with the charging cords. I did carry a charger for both
types of Iphone and microusb in the event a passengers phone was
dying.
People will really appreciate you having the charging cables.

TEXT REPLACEMENT – TEXT SHORTCUTS

To keep myself safe on the road, I developed a series of text
message shortcuts that I found myself often using. Instead of
having to pull over and compose an entirely new text message, I
could send it with the press of three keys. The following are
examples of my pre-set messages and when and why I would use

them. Remember, don't bug the passengers, 1-2 text is plenty before arrival and another 1-2 if you are waiting on them.The message, I could send it with the press of three keys. The following are examples of my pre-set messages and when and why I would use them. Remember, don't bug the passengers, 1-2 text is plenty before arrival and another 1-2 if you are waiting on them.

#

111 Hello! This is Christoph...

123 hello! this is your   ...

222 ***I am out front   In...

333 My apologies but the e...

444 In order to expedite yo...

555 Thank you for being a...

666 Unfortunafely, I cannot...

777 There is a heavy amou...

888 Which side of the stre...

999 I am terribly for the inc...

Edit

●○○○○
6:42 PM
79%
New Message
Cancel
To:
Thank you for being a 5 st...   ×
555
Send
1 2 3 4 5 6 7 8 9 0
- / : ; ( ) $ & @ "
#+= . , ? ! ' ⌫
ABC 🎤 space return

111 –"Hello, This is "your name" your friendly driver! In order to best facilitate your request, what house/address/location are at so I may find you? I will be arriving in 2015 Black Honda Accord Hybrid shortly after sending this text!"

The reasoning behind this text is that sometimes only an address range shows up. Sometimes its correct, many times the pax is a block or two over. Sending this gives them the opportunity to give you their exact address to not waste each other's time.

123- "Hello! This is your Driver, where can I find you?"

I would send this text upon arriving at a destination and it appeared to be wrong, or the client was not where they had stated they were.

It is also a nice way of saying "hurry up".

222- "I am out front in the 2015 Black Honda Accord with the Hazard lights on! =) "

I used this as my arrival text after 2 minutes. It let the passenger know what car to look for and where. I used this mainly in residential areas, or any pickup where I was 100 percent certain of the address that came through.

333- "My apologies but the exact address did not come through, can you please provide it? "

This text was used en-route when I just had an address range or it said drive to pin. I used this to get the clients exact location.

444- "In order to expedite your trip, please enter the destination address into the rider app or have physical address for the driver."

When I was halfway to the passengers' pick-up location, if I did see they had entered a destination, I would send this so we did not sit and wait while the passenger digs up the address. This is helpful when its busy and you don't have time to enter the address into the GPS when you pick them up.

555- "Thank you for being a 5 star passenger today! We appreciate your business! Have a great day!"

I sent this text out at the end of every ride for every passenger I issued a 5 star rating. More in this near the end of the book.

666- "Unfortunately, I cannot locate you, please feel free to re-request a trip when you are ready/available."

After 5 minutes of waiting or looking for the pax, I would send this message after making the last phone call trying to find them. 777- "There is a heavy amount of traffic from here to your pick-up location. For you to receive the best and fastest service, you can cancel this trip and find a car that is closer to you."
I would send this text only if there was too much traffic and it was going to take me longer than 15 minutes to arrive. Reason being, people would cancel on me when I tried without saying anything. This way, you give them the cancel option before they get charged the fee and before you go through all the stress of driving there for possibly nothing as I have had a cancel once when I was only three blocks away and I had drove 20 minutes to get there
888- "Which side of the street are you on and what is nearby?"
This is a text I would send if I could not find the pax at the address or if I was approaching a busy downtown core with one-way streets so I could avoid having the client have to cross the street to find me.
999- "I am terribly sorry for the inconvenience."
This is my reply to any complaints I received via text while en route, or for any general inconvenience.
These are the texts I used and not always. It just depends on the situation, you do not want to over-text the client but you also don't want to be lost looking for them. It also keeps your status as a safe driver as opposed to one who is texting and driving.

FIRST CALL

Greet the pax by ASKING their name and ensure they ordered the ride and it matches the ride account. Quickly confirm the address of the drop-off. After that, always ask them "How was your day/evening?" 90 percent will ask back and always say "great or excellent". This sets the tone for a pleasant ride and remember, the pax do not want to hear your problems. They may vent to you, they are paying YOU to drive, not to be your counselor. You should accept as many calls as possible in order to maximize your revenue.
However there are some things to quickly check before accepting that request:

How far is it? If it is 15 minutes away it might not be worth your time if it is only a minimum fare. Also a ride that far is likely to cancel on you if they have a low rating.

Rider rating: pay attention to rider ratings. They are there for a reason. A low rated rider is more likely to cancel on you on your way, trash your car or give you an unpleasant experience. There are the types of riders that will call for a car 15 minutes away when you have gotten almost halfway there. High rated riders, 4.6 or higher, are less likely to give you any issues.

So you've decided to accept the first ride.

The rider will be notified you are on your way by the rideshare app.

I personally created shortcuts on my Smartphone to send out text messages to my pax to avoid confusion during pick-ups.

The first I send is right as I accept. I programmed it as "111" shortcut stating the following to the passenger "This is Joe, your rideshare driver. I am en route to the destination entered in the app. I will be arriving in a black Honda Accord Hybrid."

70 percent of your passengers will be ready or coming out as you arrive if it is in the morning or busy.

Remember time is money, if the pax or passenger is not ready when you arrive after a couple of minutes I would send a text "this is your rideshare driver, I am out front of 325 main st. in the black Honda accord with my hazard lights on."

This gives them the opportunity to advise you if they are running late or you are at the correct location, as unfortunately, sometimes the pin is dropped in the wrong spot and are really 3 blocks over. If they are only a couple blocks away, just drive over to get them. If you have waited 5 minutes without word from the passenger call them. If you do not reach them, tell them "this is your rideshare driver, I am sorry I we missed you today, please request our services when you are ready". Cancel the trip and move on in this scenario.

Make sure to wait the amount of time required by your company to get the cancel fee.

WAITING/DRIVING

You will want to wait somewhere legal. Remember you are not a police car; you do not get to break the law. Make sure you are in legal waiting or loading zone, not double-parked or blocking traffic.

While rude road manners are something passengers will make note of, some passengers will wait in totally illegal places. Do not hold up traffic or risk a ticket for this. Simply circle the block, call them and advise them to move to a loading or waiting area where you can safely pick them up. Remember you are NOT a taxi and you cannot just stop in the middle of an avenue!

Once your passenger shows, get out and open the door if you can. If the road is too busy, do not risk your life. If the passengers look as if they might require some assistance, ask them instead of sitting on your phone in your car.

Once the passengers are in the car tell them your name and ASK theirs. Do not GIVE them the account name; ever, always ask for it.

This is the best way to verify you have the right person in your car. Do not leave until you have verified this.

Make sure everyone is seat belted according to your state laws and ask the passenger what their destination is. If it already shows up, verify it with them. Once you have verified the drop off point, start the ride and go.

Use a navigation system. Always. This way there isn't a dispute between you and the passenger about the route. Ask them if they have a preferred route, most likely they don't but they will tell you if they do.

You will get requests to go to the grocery store….Remember you get paid for time and miles, and mostly miles, so the longer you sit, the less you make. Anything over 3 minutes isn't worth it, and the pax can call another car without costing them extra. If a pax is going grocery shopping make sure they take all of their items with them, you do not want to have to return the items if you have an emergency. In general, it is good practice to NOT wait while people shop. They should be ordering a ride to and then from, unless it is a rural area where they might not get another car for hours.

My first and last grocery experience was a..disaster of sorts. I took
the pax to the grocery store a mile uphill and waited for 30
minutes for them..I took them back down the hill to their airbnb…I
helped them unload the groceries, and not even a single tip or
much of a thank you, it was like they expected it, and for nothing.
No thanks! You are a driver not a personal assistant! Since the
wait time of 5 minutes is usually the same as the base fare, just
explain to them that calling another car is far more economical for
them.
Many, especially late night pax will request drive thru on the way
home… Remember time and miles…. But do you want a one star
for refusing? How to avoid this? You could end up in a 20 minutes
line, and for me personally, I do not allow eating in the car. This
is a personal judgment call, I usually tell them there is no eating
allowed in the car and I will take them if the line is not long, if it
is, they can call another car to pick them up and take them home. I
honestly just stopped driving after midnight to avoid the whole fast
food scenarios. I had one during the day, they told me " a taxi
will" I told them " the taxi gets $1 per minute to wait, I get .25
cents, I am very sorry but it is not economical for me.." They told
me to skip it and they didn't leave a bad rating. But always bear in
mind your ratings may depend on silly things and this is one of
them.

PICKUP AND DROPOFF

While some of this may be common sense or review, you have no
idea how many times to this day I encounter this things. Rideshare
is not a special license to stop anywhere or drive anyway, you are
not a special vehicle, you do not have the same rights as a taxi and
many of the following practices lead to huge rises in traffic
congestion which means: less money for you….
Cities like Las Vegas have designated pick up and drop off zones.
USE THEM, they help traffic move and flow! Many cities do not,
but you cannot wait in taxi lanes or zones, you need to wait in
proper areas and not just stop in the middle of the road and drop
people off, it is illegal and dangerous for everyone around you!
You may see others do it, but it doesn't make it legal.

Driving in Seattle is a NIGHTMARE because there's little traffic enforcement and every entitled prius will just STOP without warning and let people in or out! Use your hazard lights BEFORE coming to a stop! This warns the driver behind you, especially at night that they need to slow down or stop. You are asking for a rear end accident if you do not use your hazards and in contributory states like California, it can be considered your fault if someone rear ends you because you failed to take safety precautions. Use loading zones or park somewhere. This is NOT a limo or taxi service and while you may feel you are going "above and beyond" you are actually training the PAX that they can get out wherever, which creates problems for the next driver that follows the rules. Pax cannot be picked up at a green light at a busy intersection! If you see them, wave and turn the corner until you can safely pull over to the next curb or loading zone. DO NOT PICK THEM UP IN THE TRAVEL LANES!! If they get hit, you can get sued, not just the company. It is good practice to keep congested traffic moving along. In short do not let people in and out in traffic! It is dangerous, illegal. If you cannot find a place to pull over, keep circling the block; the pax can see you in the app. Do not sit there and impede traffic illegally for 5 minutes! This creates a dangerous and non-profitable situation for everyone. Find a spot, driveway or keep circling until they come out.

POOL OR COMBINED ECONOMY RIDES

Since our last publication, carpool type services have been offered in many markets. It's been popular with riders, but not with a lot of the drivers. They allow, for a greatly reduced rate, for you to pick up multiple passengers. You will receive a trip request for PAX A, then PAX B, and the service will try to send them on a similar route. Sometimes PAX A will be the last to drop off, it all depends on the route. When you arrive, confirm 2 things: did they pax order the pool service? How many riders do they have? Put the correct number of PAX and start the trip. It is best to drop them off in the app order, do not take the pax directions because if could cause someone else to wait longer than they should. Follow the destination in the app as riders may be added as riders leave.

The app will automatically add them. I once had a 2-hour trip with multiple pax, to me it kind of felt impersonal like driving a bus. IF you want to stop this, you can hit the "stop new requests" and it will stop adding riders and you will go offline after. Remember two things: You need to go back online after to pick up anymore riders and if you stop requests during a trip, it can count against you when it comes to bonuses that require "consecutive rides" or other bonuses that may be available in your area.

TALKING TO YOUR PASSENGERS

Your passengers do not always want to hear your life story. This is their ride not yours. Gauge your passengers. Do not talk to them when they are on their phone talking or speaking to another passenger.

My approach was always to ask them how their morning/evening was going. Based on how they respond will tell you if they want to continue the conversation. If they say they are good and do not ask you how you are, they don't want to talk to you. If they ask how you are, tell them and throw something neutral in like "it is nice weather today". After that, you'll either hear more from them or total silence. It isn't usually much in between.

FOLLOW YOUR ROUTE

Pay attention to where you are going. Avoid congested or construction routes. But always take the fastest most direct route. If you miss a turn, take the next one immediately. Apologize for missing the turn and proceed to the route.

ACCEPTANCE RATE

Most companies require a strict acceptance rate. For example, 90 percent acceptance means you need to pick up 9 out of 10 calls. Adherence to this rule is a major player in keeping your eligibility for bonuses.

Remember it is an average over a period of time.

NO-SHOW / CANCEL

If you happen to be waiting for over 5 minutes with absolutely no word from your client, there is the chance of a no show. Or in the rare event they ask you to cancel. In either scenario, you will advise the client via voice message you are sorry you missed them. You will go to the app a mark them as a "no-show". In the event the rider requests the cancellation, hit "cancel – rider request" after calling them.

Once you accept a trip you can cancel it at any time. Be careful not to accept rides just to cancel them. Your company may monitor this action and find it to be out of compliance. If you have an emergency, and cannot make it to the passenger, advise them and then cancel.

WRONG PICK-UP

You might ask how this happens. It does, not often but especially when it is busy and at night. A wrong pick-up can be a simple mistake or huge disaster. I once picked up a couple on a busy avenue in the rain. Their name matched so I pulled away. My phone started ringing, it was the passenger line. It was my client calling. It turns out the passenger did not hear my name and assumed I was their ride. Since it was only two blocks in this case I circled back, dropped them off to find their driver and proceeded to find my client, which I didn't. The client left me a 1 star, even though they did not ride with me. The company told me it counted and could not be removed.

At times, the GPS can be off or the passenger may have dropped the pin in the wrong place. They may have just moved to the area. Or they may have moved from the original location from where they requested. In any case if they are not far, go pick them up and apologize for the misunderstanding. Things happen, as long as the passenger is cool about it, the ride will go fine.

RIDESHARE JACKING

Late at night in busy areas, it can be common for intoxicated people to try to convince you to drive them with cash or their account.

Always remember that this is illegal and there is a lot to lose if you are caught.

Always make sure they order through the app. Also, people at night will try to say they are the account holder. I never kept my phone where they rider could see the account name. But people will try and ride as long as they can on someone else's account until the trip ends suddenly while you are driving. The thief will pretend they don't know what to do. The first thing to do is call the passenger phone. If it does not go to their phone, you can ask them to get out of the car for theft of service.

THE RIDE

Your time to shine is now. Passengers pay attention to how you drive, so drive professionally and smoothly. Not too fast or slow without any sudden unnecessary maneuvers. If you wish or need to speed excessively to get someone to the airport, while it's totally not advisable to speed, if you are going to, ask the passenger if they would like you to HURRY. But remember: The speeding ticket is not worth the $30 fare. Drive as lawfully as you can. During the ride if they passenger is quiet let them be. They do not want to hear your life s necessarily. I found the more I talked in the morning; the more I got rated down. The quieter I was, the better rating I had. But it really came down to feeling out who wanted to talk and who did not.

SMOKING

There is no smoking in TNC vehicles in almost every state in the United States. You are totally within you rights to advise your passenger not to smoke.

HANDLING PASSENGERS

Arguing with the passenger is the quickest way to one star. Never argue with the passenger, even if they are not correct, Even if it is about the route. I found when I took the passengers wrong route that in the end, they would admit fault and not blame me for taking them out of their way. Remember if there is a disagreement, you can cancel to avoid the one-star rating.

You will have many types of passengers depending on the day from all walks of life. Everyone should be treated with the same dignity and respect always.

However, there are certain passengers that will create "patterns " in your work.

The silent passenger – The person who gives their name destination and a grating silence during the entire ride. They will look at you every now and then in the rearview but never saw anything. I cannot tell you how fast I wanted to get to the destination because of this.

Students – During the day, most students are going around campus.

This means they are usually a minimum fare ride. We will go into why minimum fare rides are not optimal later.

Business people – You would think you worked for their company given the amount of info they are discussing in the back of your car.

What is worse is when it is 3 people talking about their co-workers.

It's a little awkward and you should probably say absolutely nothing.

The fighting couple- you pick up a couple from dinner or the theatre.

You can tell by the look on one of their faces it was not an enjoyable experience. After you take off they start arguing in the backseat. It doesn't matter what it is about but as long as it is not extremely loud or threatening it is none of your business. If it becomes distracting however, remember, you are the driver and you can advise them to keep the noise down by simply saying.

"Excuse me, I am so sorry, but could we keep the decibel level down please for optimal concentration. " This way you have been more than polite and now they are worried you might run off the road so they quiet down. As soon as they realize the ride is fine, they realize they were the problem.

The chatty passenger- we mean chatty as in gasping for air. This passenger wants to talk the entire way and you may or may not. The good thing is you do not have to per say, you can "uh huh" them or you can totally engage. It is your call and one I took on a case-by case basis. If I did not have something to say back to the passenger, I would respectively nod my head that I heard them, but said no more.

I am late for my flight – We all love airport calls. Smooth, long ride.

Nice fare. Wait your flight is in an hour???!! Oh yes! Especially early in the am! The first thing to ask them is: are you checking any luggage as you hurry to the airport. The second is "are you checked in to your flight?" The airline has a bag and passenger cut off time.

For baggage it is 45 minutes-1 hour before departure time and for people with carry-on only, it is 30 minutes before take off. If the passenger has not checked in, even if they are not checking a bag if they cannot check in via mobile, they may miss the airport cut-off time. In which case the airline cannot just simple "reprint" a boarding pass, they have to put them onto the next flight. During this process, you will be the first person that comes to mind if you promised to get them there in time. Always take the pax and hurry, never tell them they will miss the flight don't bother. The airlines policies are usually such that if the passenger is at least present while they are missing their flight or show up right after, they will put them on the next one. It depends on the airline but they main point is don't ask these questions BEFORE leaving. Ask them as you are barreling down the freeway.

With these late passengers or any late passengers. Always tell them

"I will do my very best" Because you cannot guarantee the arrival time. There may be factors along the way out of your control.

Overly touchy passengers- Obviously the passengers should not be touching you, but if they have an affinity for each other, and it bothers you, remember, it is your car. This is on a driver-by-driver basis but for me, anything more than a kiss and a hug was not happening in my back seat

Intoxicated Passengers - Your biggest moneymaker but sometimes your worst nightmare. I stopped driving in the evening just to avoid them. Intoxicated passengers can be totally chill or a total nightmare. I once had to exit one from my vehicle for trying to take the wheel on the interstate because he thought it would be "cool".

When the bars let out this is one of the most difficult scenes to deal with. Severely drunken people have no concept of where to stand when being picked up. They will call from the most packed street in front of the bar for door service. Even when there are literally 100 cars blocking the road, they still will. I always tried to approach from a side street and park as close as I could to the main drag if it was gridlock. I would text the passenger my location and if no response then I would then call the passenger. If the passenger did not answer I left a message and I would wait the 5.5 minutes to cancel if it was non-surge. If the surge was on, I did not wait. How on earth am I to find them in a sea of people if they aren't answering? Besides they can get another car in less then a few minutes, as this is where all the drivers will be that do not have a passenger. So do not feel bad, if you cannot find them, cancel and wait for the next. I recommend keeping the parking spot if it is working out until the next call.

Now, if you finally found your intoxicated passenger here is what happens next.

They get in the car. You drive.

Well for the most part. You need to pay close attention when speaking to them as to how intoxicated they might be. Why? You do not want them throwing up or causing a scene in the vehicle. Both are very, very bad for your business.

It is your choice in whether or not to take an overly intoxicated person. They can become violent and threaten the safe operation of the vehicle. Or they may pass out only to throw up all over your car, and the cleaning fee isn't worth it.

At any rate, if it seems like a go, remember to crack the window a bit. There is nothing like stale air to make drunks people heave faster. If someone falls asleep while you are driving open the window more. I had a girl that got in, sounded just fine. Fell asleep and a few blocks from her destination woke up and hurled vomit all over the backseat. It was my last night driving late at night. I now cut it off at 10 – 12. I will drive people TO the bar, but I no longer pick them up. I leave that to the new drivers.. Drunken people tend to give the lowest ratings because they think they are sending a message to the company about the pricing. However unfortunately it only dents the drivers rating.

If the passenger is too intoxicated and you feel it could be unsafe, it is better to cancel the trip than be sorry. I once had two passengers, standing 7 feet from the car, and they could not find it. I called them and I saw them look around, look at the car, and then tell me they couldn't find it. They were so drunk they needed to hold each other up. In the past I had gone above and beyond only to be burned by intoxicated passengers. They promised to behave and did not at all.

So in this case, I took the call, I had tried to contact them, but if they were too drunk to find me, what was the situation going to be like in the car? I cancelled the trip, went offline and went home. Sometimes that extra $20 fare can end up being more costly if the rider causes issues.

The turn-by-turn directions passenger- Down to which lane you should be in I found this to very, very annoying and distracting. I did grit my teeth the entire rides but I said nothing. After all, I did ask if they had a preferred route… ;)

PASSENGER SCENARIOS

You are driving to pick up "Dan". You pull up to the address and wait, no answer. Your phone rings, it is "Dan", he says he is a few blocks away by the bank, what do you do?

A). Tell Dan he needs to call another car.
B.) Ask Dan which bank and which cross streets and pick him up
C.) Hang up and drive to the nearest bank
D.) Tell Dan there will be a $5 cancellation fee

You have been waiting for passenger "Kim" for 5 minutes now, you text and "Kim" says, "I will be right out". What do you do?

A.) Advise "Kim" it has been 5 minutes and she needs to call another car (collect the cancel fee)

B.) Replies back "ok" and wait another 5 minutes.

C.) Cancel the trip and leave

D.) Tell "Kim" to hurry up

The answer is B. If you have communicated with the passenger, wait for them for a reasonable amount of time. Up to 10 minutes is reasonable, especially if it is busy.

Passenger "will" shows up at 123-178 3rd avenue, not an approximate address, it is a busy avenue, what do you do?

A.) Park by 123 3rd avenue and wait

B.) Drive around the block until you see someone staring at their phone

C.) Text the passenger, ask them which side of the road they are on and if they can move to a loading zone

D.) Call the passenger right away

The answer is C. Make sure the passenger is ready for you to ensure a smooth pick up

Passenger "Glenda" comes out of her house with a suitcase in hand, what do you do?

A.) Sit and wait in the car until she gets in

B.) Get out of the car, take her luggage and put it in the trunk and open her door

C.) Open her door for her

D.) Advise her that suitcases are not allowed.

The answer is B. Go the extra mile for the passenger

Passenger "Debbie" has 4 friends she wants to pile in your sedan after the bar, but you only have 4 seatbelts. The passenger assures you her dad is the sheriff and there will be no issue, what do you do?

A.) Ask the passenger if they could possible call for a second car as you legally cannot carry them

B.) Let them pile in.

C.) Tell her that one girl has to ride in the trunk
D.) Advise her that you cannot take them and cancel.
The answer is A. IN MOST CASES. You want to be of "service" but remember, if you refuse her even partially, the rating, might be low, now what Use your best judgment between A and C. Sometimes you might want to advise them to take an extra capacity vehicle rather than taking the hit.
You are driving around looking for your passenger when you see a woman standing with her dog, you just vacuumed your car, what do you do?

A.) Politely inform the woman that you do not accept pets
B.) Keep driving like you never saw her and cancel.
C.) Accept the ride and have a blanket ready for the dog.
D.) Call the woman and tell her to order another car and cancel.
The answer is C. Since you have no idea whether the dog is a working animal for the blind or a therapy pet, either way, the Americans with disabilities act requires that you do NOT refuse them service. You can never refuse a disabled person service so long as they and their accessibility device can fit in your vehicle without cost or alteration. Treating disabled passengers differently than others can be a crime. Be sensitive to peoples needs.
You are on a stop your passenger requested. They have been gone for 20 minutes longer than they had said they would. You text and call, there is no answer, what do you do?
A.) Keep waiting, they will show eventually
B.) Call the passenger, leave them a voicemail that in a certain amount of time you will have to cancel the trip and report them as missing to the company.
C.) Drive around the block to rack up more fare
D.) Park the car and try to find the passenger
The answer is B. The passenger could be in numerous situations and it is not our job to determine what that is. Do not involve yourself, simply leave a message and leave an email to support to advise them that the passenger has abandoned their ride.

STRATEGY – HOW TO MAKE MONEY

Like any game, you need a strategy to win. Driving downtown and turning on the app might work at first but you will soon find it is not that easy. Reason being is that new drivers do that and it over saturates the area with them. You need to know where to pick up your riders and when. A good tactic is to note where you drop your passengers off or ask where they are going at night. This tells you where to pick up people later.

Mornings- When I say morning I mean 3am- 11am. Between 3am- 6am, most people are heading to the airport to catch early morning flights. Play your cards right and you can get 3 trips in before 7 am.

Every morning and especially Monday I would be on the road by 330am, approx 45 miles north of the airport, or the end of the metro area. Now normally you put yourself in unavailable mode on the freeway during the day to avoid unwanted pick ups that are too far, but at this time, they only people calling are those needing a ride to the airport. So I would troll down the freeway like a boat with a reel cast and drive until I snagged someone and then drove them to the airport.

Picking up at the airport depends on your city and if it's a grey area, don't do it, they can impound your car for it. If you can then obviously you get your next fare here.

If you are like me, our city still has no agreement, so that means dead-heading from the airport back to a desirable point. If I got the first passenger by 4, I could drive up about 30 miles from the airport and repeat the cycle until 7 am hit. Always pass by the hotels but don't depend on them, most of my fares came from private homes usually in upper class areas.

Upon dropping off near to 7 am, I would face the rush hour stream of traffic into downtown and it would provide a nice break, but in my car.

I would then drive around to neighborhoods close to downtown to pick up people going to work. Neighborhood to office, rinse and repeat until about 10am. After 10 am, the amount of rides really leveled off and I was beat. It made for the end of my shift on the weekday morning.

Evenings- M-Th ridership did not pick up until about 330pm where
I drove. The busiest hours were 7-9 AM and 5-7 PM. So you work your schedule around either of these "busy times" to maximize your efforts.
In the evening you can expect to be picking people up from work from 4-6pm and after that you will be taking people out for dinner or drinks until about 11 or so. People tend not travel a long distance on
a work night so waiting around for last call isn't really worth it unless it's a big city.
Friday, Saturday Night and Sunday – This is where the bulk of the money comes from. Friday and Saturday night people want to go out in droves. During the day people like to enjoy their weekend. Friday night is usually the busiest night of the week, but it can always be replaced by Saturday depends on what is going on. Sunday is usually pretty consistent, but if you are planning on driving at 330am
Monday, remember to get enough sleep.
The trick is to find the places where you find the riders the easiest and fastest. I grew to like driving people to the airport in the am over the evening crowd. So my strategy was after the first drop off, to take the freeway up to a residential area and drive its arterials towards the downtown hotels until I got a passenger. It worked every time, but every time someone came from a different location.
It was always seemingly random, but my consistency got me consistent earnings, and that is what mattered the most.
Get a map of the most densely populated areas of your city. Study that along with the city knowledge. The more densely populated the area, the better chance you have of picking someone up. In the am I would go from the airport to densely populated residential area. In the evenings I would go from densely populated neighborhoods to the pax destination then back again, over and over sometimes.

FARES AND PAYMENTS

The issue of how you are paid had become a very big issue for many drivers. It is the #1 complaint I see online, the misunderstanding of the payment contract. Firstly your pay structure depends on the company, and market you drive in. You, as a driver, are contracted to be paid by "time and mileage", which again varies by region. Some have a base or pickup fare along with time and miles, some do not. You are NOT paid a percentage of what the rider pays, no matter what the rider pays to the rideshare company.
The whole notion that the company is "taking" over 50 percent of the "fare" is not correct as your contract is for the distance and time you drove and any bonuses. That is it. End of story, case closed there is no mystery and they companies are very upfront about it. If you have payment questions, or feel you were shorted, always contact the rideshare company. Drivers on Facebook or other chat groups cannot help you and often drive in different areas and conditions, so the pay does VARY but usually from place to place and for the amount of time you are willing to put in.

You want the largest and fewest fares you can. It saves time, money and wear and tear on your car. This is another reason I did airport runs. Hanging around downtown will get you minimum fare trips, which when you deduct commission and expenses and extra rider fees, is less than half of what it was. On a longer fare the hit is not so bad, but how do you ensure a longer fare? While it is never possible to guess where the passenger is going, a balance of airport rides and rides to work would net me a couple hundred dollars in the am if I worked 8 hours. To avoid the short rides, I would put myself in unavailable mode and out some distance between me and where people where going. I would try to drive out far enough to get $10 fares at the minimum.
The morning is more predictable for this since 95 percent of people are going to work so they are usually headed downtown. The evening was always totally unpredictable and you need to be very prudent and patient during stop and go traffic. If it is the norm

in your city, the passengers know, they forgive you as long as you don't miss a crucial turn. But always, at least once, apologize for the traffic. It helps the passenger know you are present and on task, and most of all paying attention.

So having read all of that, you say, " I am confused, where should I be at 330am??" How do I get the longer fares?

Here is an example using a couple of cities.

AM

At 330 am you should be in a neighborhood, say, Plano slowly heading towards downtown Dallas. If you have no one by downtown you can drive over to downtown forth worth or back towards Plano.

Either way you will get a passenger within 30 minutes for certain needing to go to DFW.

In Seattle, a more north –south city, you would want to not be in Seattle proper, you would start in Lynnwood driving down interstate 5 at the speed limit or 5 under to troll for passengers. If you for some reason you make it all the way downtown with no one, simply turn around and repeat. However once you have received your first pax you only have 1-2 more you can get to sea-tac before 7. After you drop off the first pax drive back towards downtown and turn the app on when you have reached downtown and drive through downtown, up capital hill and then across to the u district. Drive across to 99 and then downtown almost like a loop. Somewhere on this loop you will get airport passenger number 2 and/or 3.

PM

I started my afternoon shifts at 3 or 4pm, enough time to prepare before rush hour. I would position myself in the parking lot of a MAJOR employer and put myself into available mode. Since I was the closest car, I always got the call. I picked companies that were downtown in which the possibility for a long distance trip was possible. It worked 99 percent of the time, I would get a fare from the company I was outside of, and since it was rush hour there was usually surge pricing, but not always. I could usually only make 1-2 trips during rush hour, which for me, ended at 7pm. After 7, I trolled the nearby neighborhoods to take people out to dinner and then later out to bars and clubs. Always remember 5 star hotels are going give you nicer riders than dive bars.

If your ride is over a certain dollar amount the fare can and is usually held for review to combat fraud. This is more common now- so expect that long ride to show up later. It is procedural, you do not need to call, it will be released once it is reviewed, just be sure to keep track of the time and mileage just in case.

EVENTS

Got a big game or concert coming to town? Chances are, people are going to need a ride!
Taking people to the stadium was never really the issue. Sure there was traffic, more than normal, but nothing like the end of the event.
The end of the event is where you really need a strategy.
You will want to know when the event ends or approximately.
There will be traffic barricades already set up, so position yourself close enough to the stadium, but close enough to the freeway/highway onramp
as possible to avoid getting stuck in the surge of traffic. For example:
In Dallas, the American Airlines arena is fairly close to 35E and 366.
You would want to wait in Victory ave by the arena so you are only two turns from 35E and 366.
In Seattle, At Safeco Field, wait across the street from home plate on S. Atlantic street where you only had to make one right turn onto highway 99 which would take me directly out of the traffic mess. NOW, the tricky part. You WANT a surge call from the event, and if you are patient, you will get it. The trick to this is, once you find your waiting location. Put yourself into unavailable. Check the rider app and wait until you see it surge past 1.5. Once you have a good surge going, put yourself in available and take the first call you can.
Advise the client where you are parked and direct them there. It is easier for them to walk to you, than for you to go to them and get stuck in traffic. Once you have taken them to their destination, go

back and see if there is anyone left, chances are, there will be
another ride waiting.
Events are a good moneymaker. You will find many riders going
out afterwards.

AIRPORTS

We have talked a lot about airport trips throughout this guide.
Airport trips are a good moneymaker, especially Monday in the
early
AM. Airport drop-offs are pretty straight forward: If you see the
passenger coming with a suitcase, get out and offer to assist them
and put the baggage away.
Confirm that they going to the airport, confirm the airline they are
taking, start the trip and ask them if they have already checked on
online. If they say "no", advise them most airlines close check in
30 minutes prior to departure, so if they have a way to check in
now, it is advisable. Reason being is if they are late, either because
they called too late or you were late, the airline can reprint a
boarding pass for an already checked in passenger to get through
security, but they cannot if they are not checked in. Also keep in
mind if they have luggage. Baggage has to travel from the counter
to aircraft and in big airports like DFW it can take 1 hour. That
means the passenger has to be physically present at the counter in
DFW 1 hour and 10 minutes prior to departure at the very
minimum or their bag may not make the flight (smaller airports
like Sea-Tac it is 45 minutes).
Passengers must travel with their bags so if they miss this cut off,
they will be put on the next fight. This is never an optimal
situation for anyone. This may seem like a lot of info for a driver,
but remember, you never want to promise something you cannot
deliver.
If the passenger calls at 6am and their flight is at 7am, you arrive
and they have luggage, which only gives you 15 minutes to get
them to the airport!! In the AM, this is doable but do advise the
passenger that you cannot guarantee it but you will try your very
best.

After you drop-off, local regulations will dictate whether you can pick up at the airport or not. Check with your local airport regulations. Picking up at the airport without authorization, can result in your car being impounded.

A lot of major cities have airport waiting lots. If the queue size is larger than 20 cars or 20 minutes, unless it is 4 -6 am it is RARELY worth waiting in the lot for an entry level ride.

SURGE/PRIMETIME PRICING

You want to wait for the surge calls that are 2x or higher during prime time. Try to wait offline until it reaches above 2x or more.Check the rider app to see where to other cars area. Remember the rider must be calling from within the surge area to get the fare. If the surge zone is small, you will find calls coming from outside the surge zone. If you have a good acceptance rate, you'll want to avoid these until you get a surge call. If you get more than 4 calls from outside the surge area, you might want to take one.

It is a careful balance to keep the balance between keeping your 90 percent and getting the surge calls. Some drivers will accept all calls, but then cancel all until they get a surge call. This strategy can get you in trouble with the company, as it can be seen as "gaming the system". In some states it has been ruled that the acceptance rate is too much like employment instead of independent contracting so the acceptance rate issue varies from state to state. I personally try to keep mine above 90 percent to qualify for bonus and promotions.

There has been a proposed change to this pricing system at the time of publishing that has not been applied to all markets and is still in test phase. Instead of using a multiplier, like 2x, 3x, it will now be fixed dollar amounts on the map. The general rules still apply but the screen will display dollars instead of multiplier. This will be somewhat of a game changer so watch the facebook group for updates.

GUARANTEED HOURLY RATES, BONUSES AND PROMOS

From time to time, or during the slow season, the company will offer hourly guarantees to make up for the lack of business and keep drivers out there. When you get the email or text for the OPT-In you should ALWAYS, ALWAYS, ALWAYS opt-in, even if you are unsure you are going to work the days shown. Opt-in and then take a screenshot of the confirmation.
The details are usually vague but usually revolve around being online
50 minutes out of the hour, accepting 1-2 rides per hour on average during a specified time. If you have any questions, email your company until its clear. Do not be afraid to email multiple times especially if you are getting conflicting answers. Remember when the company says 50 minutes online, they mean it down to 1000th of a second. I know a guy that did not get his entire weekly guarantee because he was offline half a second too long. Half a second.
The most common complaint I hear about this is using the restroom.
It is really simple. Take the call, use the restroom and go to the passenger. As long as you have sent the text that you are one your way and you are 3 minutes tops they will never even notice.
If the period is long, you may want to elect one of the hours as a break and go offline at a minute after and online a few minutes before the next hour.
If it is really slow and you are on a guarantee, move to a location where you will get short rides like a college area. Short trips in this case are better than blowing the entire weekly guarantee.
The guarantee will be an amount of fares per hour. But it is not in addition to your fares; it is to make your fares up to that amount per hour. So for example, the amount is $30 per hour. If you get one ride for $5 that hour, the company will top off the remainder. Meaning on your check they will add the DIFFERENCE of $25. If you made more than the guarantee amount, the companies will not

payout anything extra. The hourly guarantee is only to make up the difference; it is not an additional payment.
Recently varies weekly promos have been offered to get drivers to a certain area, at a certain time. Some cities offer weekly promos – some worth it, some not. 20 rides for $30? It isn't worth going out of your way for… I will accept these if I am already in the area. Some are $8-$12 for say "3 consecutive rides" in a highlighted area. This again is a way for the rideshare company to get you in a certain area, at a certain time without classifying you as an employee… I happen to live an hour drive from downtown; I would need to drive empty for an hour just to be in the area to even qualify for this type of bonus. If traffic is heavy, it just is not worth it for me and I will take rides towards downtown and if I get the bonus I do and if not, I am still out making money. Some Bonuses require a high amount of rides, combined with driving during "peak" hours and in certain areas. It is worth it if you drive full time and during rush hours or are willing to. Regardless of the promo, it is important to SCREENSHOT the promo and it's rules to make sure you follow them. You may find later you did not get the bonus. If you do not have a screenshot of the promo, it will difficult to dispute.

CANCELLATIONS EN ROUTE

Passengers cancel. It happens. It's annoying, especially if you are halfway or almost there. You just have to tell yourself, it wasn't meant to be and move on.

CLEANING FEES

Passengers are advised in the fine print that if they cause any damage to the car, they are held responsible. Any mess passengers create in your car from spilt water to vomit warrant a cleaning charge. Here is the process from which you handle it.

Put yourself into unavailable mode for an hour after. The company may not pay the fee if you do not. They are paying to clean it and your loss of business. So if you can operate with it, they may not deem the payment necessary.

Once you are offline, take photos and report it through the proper channel to the company ASAP. The company will evaluate the mess and add a cleaning fee anywhere from $50-$200 to your next paycheck.

A good way to avoid people throwing up in your vehicle is to keep plastic bags in the trunk and put them in the backseat pockets once you have decided to drive past the witching hour. A water spray bottle is also a good idea but you shouldn't need to carry an entire detail kit.

You want to report any damages to the company immediately. Serious damage like drunken riders keying your car and ruining your paint, need to be reported immediately so the rider can be indentified. This is why it is important to actually get out of your seat and do a visual walk around of your car after EACH ride. If you fail to notice, days pass, it will become impossible to know who it was and the responsibility will fall onto you.

ACCIDENTS

I have never remotely come close to having an accident with the passenger in the car. Unless you have commercial insurance, your personal policy is most likely not paying for any damages and may even drop you if you report it to them. Either way, ask the passengers if they need you to call 911. Check if they are ok. Do not get out of your seat and start running around. If your car was impacted by another vehicle you should call 911 and go to a hospital to be checked out. If you wait and you were injured, the payout from your insurance is likely to be a lot lower. Make sure your passengers are taken care of and the incident was reported to the company through their proper channel, by phone or email as soon as you can.

If the passengers want to go and call another car, certainly let them.
It is their life and their health, unless they are visibly injured, they are usually free to go once the police have taken their statement. Do not leave the scene and just email. This can be considered illegal in some places. If it was just a minor fender bender, no one was injured and you decide not to call 911, make sure you collect the other drivers' insurance information.

ABUSE

As an independent contractor you do not have to drive anyone anywhere is the attitude carried by most drivers. That you can cancel on anyone. However, you should really check your local regulations to see how strict that is. A cancel may be considered unlawful. For example, canceling all rides in the Bronx because of its geo-location (poverty, crime) until you get to Manhattan is illegal by
New York City TNC guidelines and can carry a fine. They refer to it was "passenger profiling". It is the same when a cab driver refuses to drive someone into Brooklyn. That is also illegal, but it happens all the time. So technically, you can cancel what you consider undesirable or low rated riders, but make sure you are doing it within the licensing laws of your market. Most TNC guidelines are such that you are to pick up anyone while you are "on-duty". This has become a grey area as Rideshare operates as an on demand service vs. the pre-booked TNC car services that existed prior. Prior to using an app, people called and the car would come. Whether it came on time or not, really depended on the reputation of the company and ultimately the driver. Taxicabs are notorious for not showing up on time.

SAFETY

A Dash cam is the #1 way you can protect yourself from hit and run drivers and false claims by riders. They protect you and the

rider from incident. Check your state and local laws, as some
require notification in the form of a sticker that they are being
recorded. Back up your rides! Many scams occur when a rider
makes a false complaint days later and the driver failed to back up
the footage. When it comes to "he said she said" the dash cam can
save your job.

You should at all times keep your vehicle locked. Especially
during busy times, people will jump into any car that appears to be
a rideshare car, especially if they are intoxicated. Only open the
doors at nice once you have verified you have the correct
passenger. It is always a good idea to keep a can of mace and your
phone out of the passengers reach.
If the rider becomes dangerous to the operation of the motor
vehicle or even verbally abusive, you can make the choice to end
the ride. I had this happen when the intoxicated passenger tried to
"jokingly" take the wheel. I gave him one warning, and he tried to
do it again like it was some kind of game. I pulled the vehicle over
on the side of the interstate and told the passenger the ride was
over. The passenger pleaded with me to continue the trip and
apologized profusely. This is where your judgment comes in. If he
exits, will I get paid? If he doesn't, he could cause another issue.
So what did I do? I took a risk because we were almost there and
close to the off-ramp.
I told the rider that if they sat in the backseat on their hands
or the entire duration in complete silence, I would finish the trip.
The rider complied and I dropped them off 7 minutes later. I then
wrote to support to document the situation in case the rider
reported a different story.
Sometimes Riders don't want to comply. If the rider is in
noncompliance or becomes abusive, pull over as soon as possible
and advise them the ride is over. Your or the rider will have to
cancel the ride. Since it is a cancel they cannot give you the bad
rating they were going to and you can be on your way to another
passenger.
Never, ever put up with abuse and always report it.

If you suspect a criminal or crime may be occurring in your car, what do you do? Your phone is in full view, what do you do? Simply stop at the nearest gas station, one that "appears" to have a bathroom..Call the police and either give them your plate and route, ask them to follow you or, wait for them to show up. If they follow you, it is less suspicious that you made the call. So if you continue the ride and get pulled over, it seems less likely you were the one who called. If you do a round trip, or multiple stops to residential places, most likely you might be shuttling a drug dealer, and if you continue, you could be considered an accomplice. Another is people who want you to transport packages without them. Airlines require the pax the travel with their bags for a reason. You should never, ever drive a package without a pax because if you are pulled over, and there are drugs, you will be held liable and prosecuted. It does not matter how much cash they offer, in fact the more, the more suspicious, do not do it. Cash fares are also illegal anyways.

EXERCISE AND WELLNESS

Sitting and driving all day is actually one of the worst jobs for your health. Driving 12 hours a day, 5 days a week can cause serious issues down the road. Doing a once around your vehicle isn't enough
to be considered "active". Most Smartphone's have a pedometer. Make sure you are walking at least 5-10,000 steps a day. I did this by sometimes running around the car and stretching in between rides. I felt better and made more money, because I was a in a better mood.

TIPS

Some companies have built in tipping and some do not. Most have tipping now, but because of the previous non-tipping some platform riders won't tip whereas others on a certain platform will usually tip since they have always had tipping as an option.

CASH FARES

Cash fares are illegal as a TNC driver in the United States. One that has prearranged payment, In this case, payment through the app, defines a TNC service. Many people will offer you cash fares just by seeing your phone in the window. Keep in mind some of them can be undercover police and the penalty wont be worth the fare.
Private clients are NOT legal..

RATINGS

You will never know who rated you what. Ratings can roll in right away or sometimes from weeks prior. It really depends on how often the rider uses the app. They have to rate their last ride before taking another. If the rider has questions about the rating system, you can advise them that anything lower than a 4 indicates a serious issue to the company and they may be contacted to find out what it was. The riders all have different ways they rate you, and you have some control over it. How fast or slow you drive, the music you play, the route you took all play into this. Try not to worry, as the rating is a rolling average. Also if the rider asks about ratings, remind them the rating system is a two way street and the riders are rated as well.

HOW TO GET 5 STARS FROM YOUR PASSENGERS EVERY TIME

Here we are, probably the entire reason you bought this guide. Never ask the rider for 5 stars; it is like asking for a tip. It is tacky, unprofessional and likely to get you a 1 star. So how do you

suggest it? Here is how I found was the best and most professional way, I usually, in a preprogrammed text I programmed to "555" on my
iphone, texted the phrase "Thank you for being a 5 star passenger, have a great day". A few times I said the phrase as they exit, but usually I sent it as a text. So how is that different than asking and why does it work?
Never underestimate the power of suggestion.
The ride was nearly perfect, the passenger opens their app and what are they going to remember if it wasn't a hideous ride? The last thing you said of course. And if you texted it to them, they can see it.
So it sticks in their mind 5 stars. The human brain then decides should they give you 5 stars or not. This keeps them from using their own scale of 1-5. It puts you between a 4 or 5. Why? Because you gave them 5 stars; you told them they were an excellent passenger, you boosted their ego, and most of the time that will be returned to you 99 percent of time. Never send that text or use that phrase if you did not give them 5 stars. That would be unethical. But never tell the passenger you gave them 5 stars just to get 5 stars.

IMPROVING YOUR RATINGS

Last summer my ratings took a dive to 4.75, not good. I could not figure out why. Maybe I was puzzled or jaded. So I decided to ask what people did to improve their ratings and the answer was crystal clear from al cities: Drive during the morning or day and avoid drunks until your rating goes up. Reason being is daytime riders are: regulars, used to the system, usually give a consistent rating.
Evening riders or more likely to be newbie's, drunk or infrequent users of the system, their ratings are less reliable. So the mount of variables was not something I had room to play with. I found by driving 3am-11am, and cutting off my weekend evenings at 10pm, my ratings did indeed go back up. In fact they went from a 4.75 to

a 4.94 within 2 months. As a means test I drove my old schedule. I found my ratings slid a bit for the week. That was when I made the decision to leave the night driving to the new drivers. Not everyone has the luxury of making their own schedule, but that is one of the perks of this gig, you can drive when you want and when you can. If you have read this guide in its entirety, you shouldn't find yourself in this situation. But as you can see from my own personal experience, it can happen to the best of us.

DEACTIVATION

If you get deactivated for low ratings you will be given a certain time period to improve them up to standard. If you find yourself in this situation, use the above suggestions for bringing your ratings up.
Remember the ratings are a rolling average, and the old ratings will roll off. Try not to stress about your ratings unless they are consistently going down. If you cannot improve your ratings and it does not meet company expectations, it is between you and the company as to whether or not you can continue.

REFERRALS

The company will give you a bonus for every new driver you refer.
At this stage in the game, it is up to you. If this is a short-term gig, by all means refer all the drivers you want. The company is eternally hiring anyways and anyone they hire directly gets no bonus. If you want to consider this as a long-term income solution remember that every new driver cuts into your income and is yet another driver to pick up your fares. The decision is up to you.

PROTECT YOUR BUSINESS

Protect your business with LLC or Corp status. Using an LLC or

Corp can have many tax as well as liability advantages. An LLC or Corp can protect you against costly lawsuits, especially if your car is owned or leased in the business name. For tax advantages, visit your local tax advisor to see how this can benefit you.

LOST AND FOUND

Some companies have a centralized lost and found and some require you to meet the passenger to return the item in which you will receive a payment. In that case you are responsible for returning the riders lost items or belongings. They are not yours to sell, and yes ebay can track down the Imei or serial numbers so don't even think about it. Most Passengers call their phone in lost or stolen when they can't get a hold of the driver. It is good practice to "sweep" the car or look through the backseat after EVERY ride to make sure nothing is left in your car. Do not expect the next passenger to find it; I have ended my night with multiple passenger items in the car! This made me check after each ride because I had 3 people to return those to!

HOW TO MAKE THE MOST MONEY WITH THE LEAST EFFORT

Refer People. Seriously. If you are an economy service driver, referrals are the best way to make money. 2 per week will usually cover 30-40 hours of driving.
Do higher end services – The way to make serious money with this is to offer the higher end services with a high-end car, SUV or Van. The Economy services can make you A thousand or two a week but you are killing your car and yourself driving. If you want to make serious money doing this, invest in a used higher end car or do referrals.

Honda and Accord are registered trademarks by the Honda Corporation, all rights

www.ingramcontent.com/pod-product-compliance
Lightning Source LLC
Chambersburg PA
CBHW051424250726
48655CB00003B/1217